CROCHET

Delma's Diagonal Stitch™

Annie's Attic • Berne, IN 46711 • DRGnetwork.com • *Delma's Diagonal Stitch* 1

General Information

Many of the products used in this pattern book can be purchased from local craft, fabric and variety stores, or from the Annie's Attic Needlecraft Catalog *(see Customer Service information on page 23).*

Contents

Diagonal Stitch Pot Holder.... 3

Diagonal Stitch Place Mat.... 4

Baby Pinwheel Afghan.......... 6

Earthly Delights Afghan........ 9

Earth & Sky Rug 12

Southwest Shawl 14

Sunny Shores
Table Runner 17

Purple Mountain Majesty
Bedspread 20

Stitch Guide 24

Diagonal Stitch Pot Holder

SKILL LEVEL

EASY

FINISHED SIZE

6¾ inches square, excluding hanging loop

MATERIALS

- ❑ Elmore-Pisgah Peaches & Crème medium (worsted) weight yarn (2½ oz/122 yds/71g per ball): 1 ball each #26 light blue and #121 chocolate

4 MEDIUM

- ❑ Size H/8/5.5mm crochet hook or size needed to obtain gauge

GAUGE

Rows 1 & 2 = 1¾ inches

SPECIAL STITCHES

Beginning diagonal stitch (beg diagonal st): Ch 6, dc in 4th ch from hook *(first 3 chs count as first ch-3 sp)*, dc in each of last 2 chs *(see row 1 on Fig. 1)*.

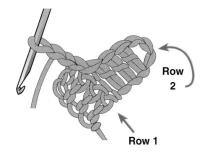

**Diagonal Stitch
Fig. 1**

Diagonal stitch (diagonal st): Sl st in next ch-3 sp *(see row 2 of Fig. 1)*, ch 3, 3 dc in same ch sp.

INSTRUCTIONS
POT HOLDER
Side
Make 2.

Row 1: With light blue, **beg diagonal st** *(see Special Stitches)*, turn.

Row 2: Beg diagonal st, **diagonal st** *(see Special Stitches)*, turn. *(2 diagonal sts)*

Rows 3–7: Beg diagonal st, diagonal st in each diagonal st across, turn. *(7 diagonal sts at end of last row)*

Rows 8–12: Sl st in each of first 3 sts, diagonal st in each diagonal st across to last diagonal st, sl st in last ch sp, turn. *(2 diagonal sts at end of last row)*

Row 13: Sl st in each of first 3 sts, diagonal st in next diagonal st, sl st in ch-3 sp of last diagonal st. Fasten off.

EDGING

Rnd 1: Holding Side pieces tog, working through both thicknesses, join light blue with sc in first st, evenly sp sc around outer edge with 3 sc in each corner, join with sl st in beg sc. Fasten off.

Rnd 2: Join chocolate with sc in first st, working from left to right, **reverse sc** *(see Fig. 2)* in each st around, join with sl st in beg sc, ch 8 *(hanger)*, sl st in same st. Fasten off. ❑❑

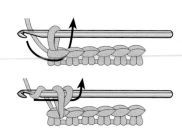

**Reverse Single Crochet
Fig. 2**

Diagonal Stitch Place Mat

FINISHED SIZE
14 x 18½ inches

MATERIALS
- ❑ Elmore-Pisgah Peaches & Crème medium (worsted) weight yarn (2½ oz/122 yds/71g per ball):
  2 balls #26 light blue
  1 ball #121 chocolate
- ❑ Size H/8/5.5mm crochet hook or size needed to obtain gauge

GAUGE
Rows 1 & 2 = 1¾ inches

SPECIAL STITCHES
Beginning diagonal stitch (beg diagonal st): Ch 6, dc in 4th ch from hook *(first 3 chs count as first ch-3 sp)*, dc in each of last 2 chs *(see row 1 on Fig. 1)*.

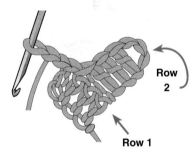

**Diagonal Stitch
Fig. 1**

Diagonal stitch (diagonal st): Sl st in next ch-3 sp *(see row 2 of Fig. 1)*, ch 3, 3 dc in same ch sp.
Beginning diagonal decrease (beg diagonal dec): Ch 3, 3 dc in same ch sp.

INSTRUCTIONS
PLACE MAT
Row 1: With light blue, **beg diagonal st** *(see Special Stitches)*, turn.

Row 2: Beg diagonal st, **diagonal st** *(see Special Stitches)*, turn. *(2 diagonal sts)*
Rows 3–6: Beg diagonal st, diagonal st in each diagonal st across, turn. At end of last row, fasten off. *(6 diagonal sts at end of last row)*
Row 7: Join chocolate with sl st in first st, beg diagonal st, diagonal st in each diagonal st across, turn. Fasten off. *(7 diagonal sts)*
Row 8: Join light blue with sl st in first st, beg diagonal st, diagonal st in each diagonal st across, turn. Fasten off. *(8 diagonal sts)*
Row 9: Join chocolate with sl st in first st, beg diagonal st, diagonal st in each diagonal st across, turn. *(9 diagonal sts)*
Row 10: Beg diagonal st, diagonal st in each diagonal st across, turn. Fasten off. *(10 diagonal sts)*
Row 11: Join light blue with sl st in first st, beg diagonal st, diagonal st in each diagonal st across, turn.
Rows 12–15: Beg diagonal st, diagonal st in each diagonal st across, turn. *(15 diagonal sts at end of last row)*
Row 16: Sl st in each of first 3 sts, diagonal st in each diagonal st across, turn.
Row 17: Beg diagonal st, diagonal st in each diagonal st across to last diagonal st, sl st in ch-3 sp of last diagonal st, turn.
Rows 18–21: [Rep rows 16 and 17 alternately] twice.
Rows 22–25: Sl st in each of first 3 sts, diagonal st in each diagonal st across to last diagonal st, sl st in ch-3 sp of last diagonal st, turn. At end of last row, fasten off. *(11 diagonal sts at end of last row)*
Row 26: Join chocolate with sl st in ch-3 sp of last diagonal st made, **beg diagonal dec** *(see Special Stitches)* in same ch sp, diagonal st in each diagonal st across to last diagonal st, sl st in ch-3 sp of last diagonal st, turn. *(10 diagonal sts)*
Row 27: Sl st in each of first 3 sts, diagonal st in each diagonal st across

to last diagonal st, sl st in ch-3 sp of last diagonal st, turn. Fasten off. *(9 diagonal sts)*
Row 28: Join light blue with sl st in ch-3 sp of last diagonal st, beg diagonal dec in same ch sp, diagonal st in each diagonal st across to last diagonal st, sl st in ch-3 sp of last diagonal st, turn. Fasten off. *(8 diagonal sts)*
Row 29: Join chocolate with sl st in ch-3 sp of last diagonal st, beg diagonal dec in same ch sp, diagonal st across to last diagonal st, sl st in ch-3 sp of last diagonal st, turn. Fasten off. *(7 diagonal sts)*
Row 30: Join light blue with sl st in ch sp of last diagonal st, beg diagonal dec in same ch sp, diagonal st across to last diagonal st, sl st in ch-3 sp of last diagonal st, turn. *(6 diagonal sts)*
Rows 31–34: Sl st in each of first 3 sts, diagonal st in each diagonal st across to last diagonal st, sl st in ch-3 sp of last diagonal st, turn. *(2 diagonal sts at end of last row)*
Row 35: Sl st in each of first 3 sts, diagonal st in next diagonal st, sl st in ch-3 sp of last diagonal st. **Do not fasten off**.

EDGING
Rnd 1: Working around edges, ch 1, evenly sp sc around with 3 sc in each corner, join with sl st in beg sc. Fasten off.
Rnd 2: Join chocolate with sc in first st, working from left to right, **reverse sc** *(see Fig. 2)* in each st around, join with sl st in beg sc. Fasten off. ❑❑

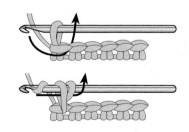

**Reverse Single Crochet
Fig. 2**

Baby Pinwheel Afghan

SKILL LEVEL
INTERMEDIATE

FINISHED SIZE
32 x 46 inches

MATERIALS
- ❑ TLC Baby light (light worsted) weight yarn (6 oz/490 yds/ 170g per ball):
    - 3 skeins #5011 white
    - 2 skeins each #7624 lime and #5730 bright pink
- ❑ Sizes D/3/3.25mm and E/4/3.5mm crochet hooks or size needed to obtain gauge
- ❑ Tapestry needle

GAUGE
Size D hook: 17 sc = 4 inches
Square = 3½ inches

SPECIAL STITCHES
Beginning diagonal stitch (beg diagonal st): Ch 6, dc in 4th ch from hook *(first 3 chs count as first ch-3 sp)*, dc in each of last 2 chs *(see row 1 on Fig. 1)*.

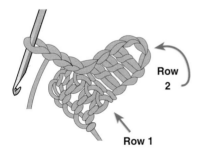

**Diagonal Stitch
Fig. 1**

Diagonal stitch (diagonal st): Sl st in next ch-3 sp *(see row 2 of Fig. 1)*, ch 3, 3 dc in same ch sp.
Beginning diagonal decrease (beg diagonal dec): Ch 3, 3 dc in same ch sp.
Invisible seam: Lay pieces to be joined edge to edge, with tapestry needle, secure yarn at top of first piece *(see Fig. 2)*, [st in 2nd piece by going in and out of edge st, stitch in same way back in first piece] across. Secure end.

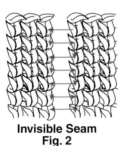

**Invisible Seam
Fig. 2**

INSTRUCTIONS
AFGHAN
Square
Make 48 bright pink and white and 48 lime and white.
Row 1: With size E hook and color, **beg diagonal st** *(see Special Stitches)*, turn.
Row 2: Beg diagonal st, **diagonal st** *(see Special Stitches)*, turn. *(2 diagonal sts)*
Rows 3–6: Beg diagonal st, diagonal st in each diagonal st across, turn. At

end of last row, fasten off. *(6 diagonal sts at end of last row)*
Row 7: Join white with sl st in ch-3 sp of last diagonal st, **beg diagonal dec** *(see Special Stitches)*, diagonal st in each diagonal st across to last diagonal st, sl st in ch-3 sp of last diagonal st, turn. *(5 diagonal sts)*
Rows 8–10: Sl st in each of first 3 sts, diagonal st in each diagonal st across to last diagonal st, sl st in ch sp of last diagonal st, turn. *(2 diagonal sts at end of last row)*
Row 11: Sl st in each of first 3 sts, diagonal st in next diagonal st, sl st in ch-3 sp of last diagonal st. Fasten off.

ASSEMBLY
With matching color yarn using invisible seam *(see Special Stitches)*, sew 4 matching Squares tog in pinwheel design *(see Fig. 3)*.

Sew tog according to Fig. 4.

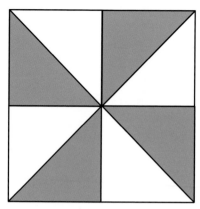

Pinwheel Square Assembly Digram
Fig. 3

EDGING

Row 1: With size E hook, join white with sc in any corner, 2 sc in same st, evenly sp sc around outer edge with 3 sc in each corner, join with sl st in beg sc, turn.

Rnds 2 & 3: Ch 1, sc in each st around, with 3 sc in each center corner st, join with sl st in beg sc, turn. At end of last rnd, fasten off.

Rnd 4: Join bright pink with sc in any center corner st, sc in each st around, with 3 sc in each center corner st. join with sl st in beg sc, turn.

Rnds 5–7: Rep rnd 2. At end of last rnd, fasten off.

Rnds 8 & 9: With green, rep rnd 4.

Rnd 10: With size D hook, ch 1, working from left to right, **reverse sc** (see Fig. 5) in each st around, join with sl st in beg sc. Fasten off. ❑❑

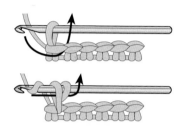

Reverse Single Crochet
Fig. 5

Baby Pinwheel Afghan Assembly Diagram
Fig. 4

SKILL LEVEL

EASY

FINISHED SIZE
59 x 75 inches

MATERIALS
- ❑ Red Heart Super Saver medium (worsted) weight yarn (5 oz/ 244 yds/141g per skein): 7 skeins #975 amazon **4 MEDIUM**
- ❑ Red Heart Classic medium (worsted) weight yarn (3½ oz/ 190 yds/99g per skein):
    - 6 skeins each #365 coffee, #336 warm brown and #334 tan
- ❑ Sizes F/5/3.75mm, G/6/4mm and H/8/5mm crochet hooks or size needed to obtain gauge
- ❑ Tapestry needle

GAUGE
Size G hook: 4 sc = 2 inches

SPECIAL STITCHES
Beginning diagonal stitch (beg diagonal st): Ch 6, dc in 4th ch from hook *(first 3 chs count as first ch-3 sp)*, dc in each of last 2 chs *(see row 1 on Fig. 1)*.

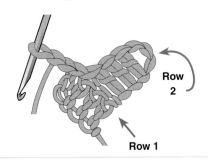

Diagonal Stitch
Fig. 1

Diagonal stitch (diagonal st): Sl st in next ch-3 sp *(see row 2 of Fig. 1)*, ch 3, 3 dc in same ch sp.

Beginning diagonal decrease (beg diagonal dec): Ch 3, 3 dc in same ch sp.

Invisible seam: Lay pieces to be joined edge to edge, with tapestry needle, secure yarn at top of first piece *(see Fig. 2)*, [st in 2nd piece by going in and out of edge st, stitch in same way back in first piece] across. Secure end.

Invisible Seam
Fig. 2

INSTRUCTIONS

AFGHAN
Square
Make 48.
Row 1: With size H hook and coffee, **beg diagonal st** *(see Special Stitches)*, turn.

Row 2: Beg diagonal st, **diagonal st** *(see Special Stitches)*, turn. *(2 diagonal sts)*

Rows 3–6: Beg diagonal st, diagonal st in each diagonal st across, turn. At end of last row, fasten off. *(6 diagonal sts at end of last row)*

Row 7: Join tan with sl st in first st, beg diagonal st, diagonal st in each diagonal st across, turn. *(7 diagonal sts)*

Row 8: Rep row 3. Fasten off.

Row 9: With amazon, rep row 7. *(9 diagonal sts)*

Rows 10 & 11: Rep row 3. *(11 diagonal sts at end of last row)*

Rows 12 & 13: Sl st in each of first 3 sts, diagonal st in each diagonal st across to last diagonal st, sl st in last ch-3 sp of last diagonal st, turn. At end of last row, fasten off. *(9 diagonal sts at end of last row)*

Row 14: Join tan with sl st in ch-3 sp of last diagonal st, **beg diagonal dec**

(see Special Stitches), diagonal st across to last diagonal st, sl st in ch-3 sp of last diagonal st, turn. *(8 diagonal sts)*

Row 15: Rep row 12. Fasten off. *(7 diagonal sts)*

Row 16: Join warm brown with sl st in ch-3 sp, beg diagonal dec, diagonal st across to last diagonal st, sl st in ch-3 sp of last diagonal st, turn. *(6 diagonal sts)*

Rows 17–20: Sl st in each of first 3 sts, diagonal st in each diagonal st across to last diagonal st, sl st in ch-3 sp of last diagonal st, turn. At end of last row, fasten off. *(2 diagonal sts at end of last row)*

Row 21: Sl st in each of first 3 sts, diagonal st in next diagonal st, sl st in ch-3 sp of last diagonal st. Fasten off.

ASSEMBLY

With matching color yarn using **invisible seam** *(see Special Stitches)*, sew Squares tog according to Fig. 3.

EDGING

Rnd 1: With size G hook, join tan with sc in any corner, 2 sc in same st, evenly sp sc around outer edge with 3 sc in each corner, join with sl st in beg sc, **turn.**

Rnds 2 & 3: Ch 1, sc in each st around, with 3 sc in each center corner st, join with sl st in beg sc, turn. At end of last rnd, fasten off.

Rnd 4: Join warm brown with sc in any center corner st, 2 sc in same st, sc in each st around, with 3 sc in each center corner st, join with sl st in beg sc, turn. Fasten off.

Rnds 5 & 6: Rep rnds 2 and 3.

Rnd 7: With coffee, rep rnd 4.

Rnds 8 & 9: Rep rnd 2. At end of last rnd, **do not fasten off.**

Rnd 10: With size F hook, working from left to right, ch 1, reverse sc *(see Fig. 4)* in each st around, join with sl st in beg reverse sc. Fasten off. ❏❏

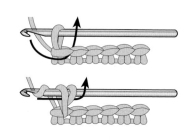

Reverse Single Crochet
Fig. 4

Earthly Delights Afghan Assembly Diagram
Fig. 3

Earth & Sky Rug

SKILL LEVEL

INTERMEDIATE

FINISHED SIZE
30 x 39 inches

MATERIALS
❑ Red Heart Grande super bulky (super chunky) weight yarn (6 oz/143 yds/170g per skein): 2 skeins each #2332 linen, #2883 country blue and #2368 dark brown

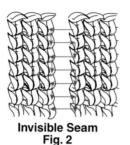

6 SUPER BULKY

❑ Sizes J/10/6mm and K/10½/ 6.5mm crochet hooks or size needed to obtain gauge
❑ Tapestry needle

GAUGE
Size J hook: 9 sc = 4 inches
Size K hook: Rows 1 & 2 = 2½ inches

SPECIAL STITCHES
Beginning diagonal stitch (beg diagonal st): Ch 6, dc in 4th ch from hook (*first 3 chs count as first ch-3 sp*), dc in each of last 2 chs (*see row 1 on Fig. 1*).

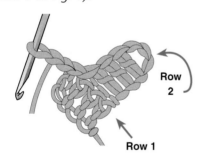

Row 2

Row 1

**Diagonal Stitch
Fig. 1**

Diagonal stitch (diagonal st): Sl st in next ch-3 sp (*see row 2 of Fig. 1*), ch 3, 3 dc in same ch sp.

Beginning diagonal decrease (beg diagonal dec): Ch 3, 3 dc in same ch sp.

Invisible seam: Lay pieces to be joined edge to edge, with tapestry needle, secure yarn at top of first piece (*see Fig. 2*), [st in 2nd piece by going in and out of edge st, stitch in same way back in first piece] across. Secure end.

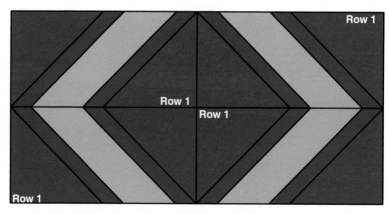

**Invisible Seam
Fig. 2**

INSTRUCTIONS
RUG
Rectangle
Make 4.
Row 1: With size K hook and country blue, **beg diagonal st** (*see Special Stitches*), turn.
Row 2: Beg diagonal st, **diagonal st** (*see Special Stitches*), turn. (*2 diagonal sts*)
Rows 3–6: Beg diagonal st, diagonal st in each diagonal st across, turn. At end of last row, fasten off. (*6 diagonal sts at end of last row*)
Row 7: Join dark brown with sl st in first st, beg diagonal st, diagonal st in each diagonal st across, turn. (*7 diagonal sts*)
Rows 8 & 9: Rep row 3. At end of last row, fasten off. (*9 diagonal sts at end of last row*)
Row 10: With linen, rep row 7. (*10 diagonal sts*)
Row 11: Rep row 3. (*11 diagonal sts*)
Row 12: Sl st in each of first 3 sts, diagonal st in each ch-3 sp across, turn.
Row 13: Beg diagonal st, diagonal st in each diagonal st across to last diagonal st, sl st in ch-3 sp of last diagonal st, turn. (*11 diagonal sts*)
Rows 14 & 15: Rep rows 12 and 13.
Row 16: Sl st in each of first 3 sts, diagonal st in each diagonal st across to last diagonal st sl st in ch-3 sp of last diagonal st, turn. Fasten off.
Row 17: Join dark brown with sl st in first ch sp, **beg diagonal dec** (*see Special Stitches*), diagonal st across to last diagonal st, sl st in last ch sp of last diagonal st, turn. (*9 diagonal sts*)
Rows 18 & 19: Sl st in each of first 3 sts, diagonal st in each diagonal st across to last diagonal st, sl st in ch-3 sp of last diagonal st, turn. At end of last row, fasten off. (*7 diagonal sts at end of last row*)
Row 20: Join country blue with sl st in ch-3 sp of last diagonal st, beg diagonal dec, diagonal st in each diagonal st across to last diagonal st, sl st in ch sp of last diagonal st, turn. (*6 diagonal sts*)
Rows 21–24: Sl st in each of first 3 sts, diagonal st in each diagonal st across to last diagonal st, sl st in ch-3 sp of last diagonal st, turn. At end of last row, fasten off. (*2 diagonal sts at end of last row*)
Row 25: Sl st in each of first 3 sts, diagonal st in next diagonal st, sl st in ch-3 sp of last diagonal st. Fasten off.

**Earth & Sky Rug Assembly Diagram
Fig. 3**

Row 1

Row 1

Row 1

Row 1

Row 1

ASSEMBLY

With matching color yarn using invisible seam *(see Special Stitches)*, sew Rectangles tog according to Fig. 3.

EDGING

Rnd 1: With size J hook, join linen with sc in any corner, 2 sc in same corner, evenly sp sc around outer edge with 3 sc in each corner, join with sl st in beg sc, turn.

Rnds 2–4: Ch 1, sc in each st around with 3 sc in each center corner st, join with sl st in beg sc, turn. At end of last rnd, **do not turn.** Fasten off.

Rnd 5: Join country blue with sc in any center corner st, 2 sc in same corner, sc in each st around with 3 sc in each center corner st, join with sl st in beg sc, turn. Fasten off.

Rnd 6: Join dark brown with sc in any center corner st, 2 sc in same corner, sc in each st around with 3 sc in each center corner st, join with sl st in beg. Fasten off. ❏❏

Southwest Shawl

SKILL LEVEL

INTERMEDIATE

FINISHED SIZE
20 x 66 inches

MATERIALS
- ❑ Elmore-Pisgah America's Best size 5 cabled crochet cotton (1¾ oz/77 yds/50g per ball):
  - 11 balls #4 ecru
  - 2 balls each #61 teak,
  - #12 rose pink and
  - #46 abbey rose
- ❑ Sizes F/5/3.75mm and G/6/4mm crochet hooks or size needed to obtain gauge

GAUGE
Size G hook: Rows 1 & 2 = 1¾ inches

SPECIAL STITCHES
Beginning diagonal stitch (beg diagonal st): Ch 6, dc in 4th ch from hook (*first 3 chs count as first ch-3 sp*), dc in each of last 2 chs (*see row 1 on Fig. 1*).

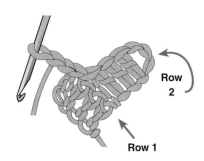

**Diagonal Stitch
Fig. 1**

Diagonal stitch (diagonal st): Sl st in next ch-3 sp (*see row 2 of Fig. 1*), ch 3, 3 dc in same ch sp.

Beginning diagonal decrease (beg diagonal dec): Ch 3, 3 dc in same ch sp.

Invisible seam: Lay pieces to be joined edge to edge, with tapestry needle, secure yarn at top of first piece (*see Fig. 2*), [st in 2nd piece by going in and out of edge st, stitch in same way back in first piece] across. Secure end.

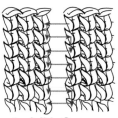

**Invisible Seam
Fig. 2**

INSTRUCTIONS
SHAWL
Rectangle A
Make 5.
Row 1 (WS): With size G hook and ecru, **beg diagonal st** (*see Special Stitches*), turn.

Row 2 (RS): Beg diagonal st, **diagonal st** (*see Special Stitches*), turn. (*2 diagonal sts*)

Rows 3–8: Beg diagonal st, diagonal st in each diagonal st across, turn. (*8 diagonal sts at end of last row*)

Row 9: Beg diagonal st, diagonal st in each diagonal st across to last diagonal st, sl st in ch-3 sp of last diagonal st, turn.

Row 10: Sl st in each of first 3 sts, diagonal st in each diagonal st across, turn.

Row 11: Rep row 9. Fasten off.

Row 12: Join rose pink with sl st in ch-3 sp of last diagonal st, **beg diagonal dec** (*see Special Stitches*) in same ch sp, diagonal st in each diagonal st across, turn. Fasten off.

Row 13: Join teak with sl st in last st of last diagonal st, beg diagonal st, diagonal st in each diagonal st across to last diagonal st, sl st in ch-3 sp of last diagonal st, turn. Fasten off.

Row 14: Rep row 12.

Row 15: With ecru, rep row 13.

Row 16: Join abbey rose with sl st in ch-3 sp of last diagonal st, beg diagonal dec, diagonal st in each diagonal st across, turn.

Rows 17 & 18: Rep rows 9 and 10. At end of last row, fasten off.

Row 19: With ecru, rep row 13.

Rows 20 & 21: Rep rows 12 and 13.

Row 22: Rep row 12.

Row 23: Join ecru with sl st in last st of diagonal st, beg diagonal dec, diagonal st in each st across to last diagonal st, sl st in ch-3 sp of last diagonal st, turn.

Rows 24 & 25: Rep rows 10 and 9.

Row 26: Rep row 10.

Rows 27–32: Sl st in each of first 3 sts, diagonal st in each diagonal st across to last diagonal st, sl st in ch-3 sp of last diagonal st, turn. (*2 diagonal sts at end of last row*)

Row 33: Sl st in each of first 3 sts, diagonal st in next diagonal st, sl st in ch-3 sp of last diagonal st. Fasten off.

Rectangle B
Make 5.
Rows 1–8: Rep rows 1–8 of Rectangle A.

Row 9: Sl st in each of first 3 sts, diagonal st in each diagonal st across, turn. (*8 diagonal sts*)

Row 10: Beg diagonal st, diagonal st in each diagonal st across to last diagonal st, sl st in ch-3 sp of last diagonal st, turn.

Row 11: Rep row 9. Fasten off.

Row 12: Join rose pink with sl st in last st of last diagonal st, beg diagonal st, diagonal st in each diagonal st across to last diagonal st, sl st in ch-3 sp of last diagonal st, turn.

Row 13: Join teak with sl st in ch-3 sp of last diagonal st, beg diagonal dec in same ch sp, diagonal st in each diagonal st across, turn. Fasten off.

Row 14: Rep row 12.

Row 15: With ecru, rep row 13.

Row 16: Join abbey rose with sl st in last st of last diagonal st, beg diagonal st, diagonal st in each diagonal st across to last diagonal st, sl st in ch-3 sp of last diagonal st, turn.

Rows 17 & 18: Rep rows 9 and 10. At end of last row, fasten off.

Row 19: With ecru, rep row 13.

Rows 20 & 21: Rep rows 12 and 13.

Row 22: Rep row 12.

Row 23: Join ecru with sl st in ch-3 sp of last diagonal st, beg diagonal dec in same ch sp, diagonal st in each diagonal st across, turn.

Rows 24 & 25: Rep rows 10 and 9.
Row 26: Rep row 10.
Rows 27–33: Rep rows 27–33 of Rectangle A.

ASSEMBLY
With matching color yarn, using **invisible seam** *(see Special Stitches)*, sew Rectangles tog according to Fig. 3.

EDGING
Row 1: Working down 1 long edge, with size F hook, join ecru with sc in corner, evenly sp sc across to next corner, do not turn.
Row 2: Working from left to right, ch 1, **reverse sc** *(see Fig. 4)* in each st across. Fasten off.

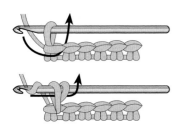

Reverse Single Crochet
Fig. 4

Rep Edging on rem long edge.

Fringe
Cut 4 strands each 20 inches in length. Holding all strands tog, fold in half. Pull fold through, pull ends through fold. Pull to tighten.

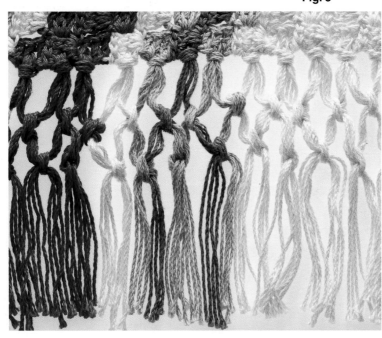

Matching colors, attach Fringe in each row across each short end.

First Row of Knots
Beg at side edge, leave first 4 strands free. [Tie next 4 strands of this Fringe and 4 strands of next Fringe tog *(see Fig. 5)* making knot 1½ inch from first knot] across, leaving last 2 sts free.

Last Row of Knots
Beg at side edge, making knot 1½ from last knot, tie knots across according to Fig. 5.
Trim ends. ❏❏

2nd Row of Knots

Knotted Fringe
Fig. 5

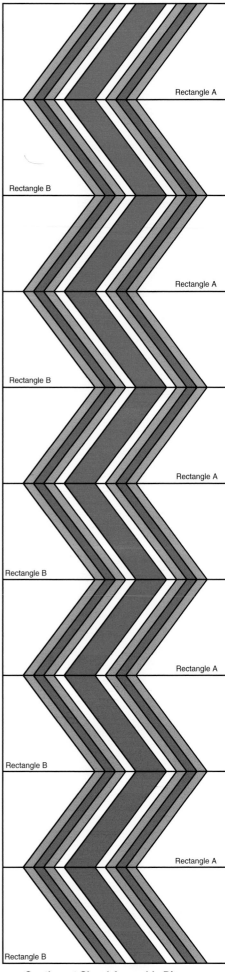

Southwest Shawl Assembly Diagram
Fig. 3

SKILL LEVEL

INTERMEDIATE

FINISHED SIZE

15 x 60 inches

MATERIALS

❑ Elmore-Pisgah Honeysuckle Yarns fine (sport) weight yarn (19½ oz/1,950 yds/ 556g per cone):
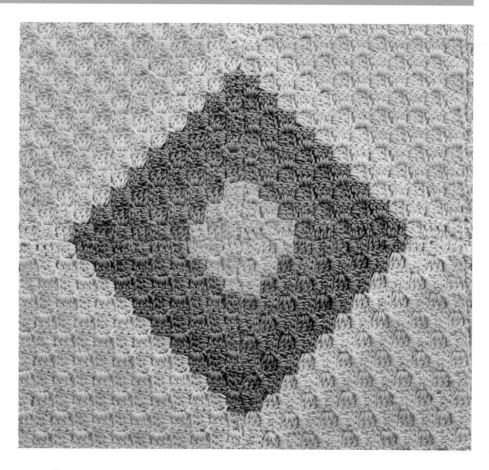

10 oz/1,000 yds/284g #1010 Daisy Mae (A)

6 oz/6000 yds/170g #104 sugar in the raw (B)

4 oz/400 yds/113g #126 sky blue (C)

2 oz/200 yds/57g #1092 army tan (D)

❑ Size C/2/2.75mm crochet hook or size needed to obtain gauge

❑ Tapestry needle

GAUGE

Rows 1 & 2 = 1 inch

SPECIAL STITCHES

Beginning diagonal stitch (beg diagonal st): Ch 6, dc in 4th ch from hook *(first 3 chs count as first ch-3 sp)*, dc in each of last 2 chs *(see row 1 on Fig. 1)*.

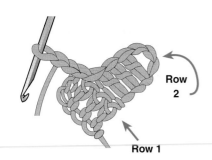

Row 2

Row 1

**Diagonal Stitch
Fig. 1**

Diagonal stitch (diagonal st): Sl st in next ch-3 sp *(see row 2 of Fig. 1)*, ch 3, 3 dc in same ch sp.

Beginning diagonal decrease (beg diagonal dec): Ch 3, 3 dc in same ch sp.

Invisible seam: Lay pieces to be joined edge to edge, with tapestry needle, secure yarn at top of first piece *(see Fig. 2)*, [st in 2nd piece by going in and out of edge st, stitch in same way back in first piece] across. Secure end.

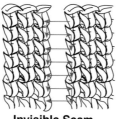

**Invisible Seam
Fig. 2**

INSTRUCTIONS

RUNNER
Rectangle A
Make 10.
Row 1 (WS): With A, **beg diagonal st** *(see Special Stitches)*, turn.
Row 2 (RS): Beg diagonal st, **diagonal st** *(see Special Stitches)*, turn. *(2 diagonal sts)*

Row 3: Beg diagonal st, diagonal st in each diagonal st across, turn. Fasten off. *(3 diagonal sts)*

Row 4: Join D with sl st in last st, beg diagonal st, diagonal st in each diagonal st across, turn. *(4 diagonal sts)*

Rows 5 & 6: Rep row 3. At end of last row, fasten off. *(6 diagonal sts)*

Rows 7–9: With C, rep rows 4–6. *(9 diagonal sts at end of last row)*

Rows 10–12: With B, rep rows 4 and 5. *(11 diagonal sts at end of last row)*

Row 13: Join A with sl st in last st of last diagonal st, diagonal st across to last diagonal st, sl st in ch-3 sp of last diagonal st, turn. *(12 diagonal sts)*

Row 14: Sl st in each of first 3 sts, diagonal st in each diagonal st across, turn.

Row 15: Beg diagonal st, diagonal st in each diagonal st across to last diagonal st, sl st in ch-3 sp of last diagonal st, turn.

Rows 16–25: Sl st in each of first 3 sts, diagonal st in each diagonal st across to last diagonal st, sl st in ch-3 sp of last diagonal st, turn. *(2 diagonal sts at end of last row)*

Row 26: Sl st in each of first 3 sts, diagonal st in next ch-3 sp, sl st in last ch-3 sp. Fasten off.

Rectangle B
Make 10.

Rows 1–12: Rep rows 1-12 of Rectangle A.

Row 13: Join A with sl st in ch sp of last diagonal st, ch 3, 3 dc in same ch sp, diagonal st in each diagonal st across, turn.

Row 14: Beg diagonal st, diagonal st in each diagonal st across to last diagonal st, sl st in ch-3 sp of last diagonal st, turn.

Row 15: Sl st across to next ch sp, **beg diagonal dec** *(see Special Stitches)* in ch sp, diagonal st in each diagonal st across, turn.

Row 16: Sl st across to next ch sp, diagonal st in ch sp, diagonal st in each diagonal st across, turn. Fasten off.

Rows 17–26: Rep rows 17–26 of Rectangle A.

ASSEMBLY
With matching color yarn using invisible seam *(see Special Stitches)*, sew Rectangles tog according to Fig. 3.

EDGING
Rnd 1: Join A with sc in any corner, 2 sc in same corner, evenly sp sc around outer edge with 3 sc in each corner, join with sl st in beg sc, turn.

Rnd 2: Ch 1, sc in each st around, with 3 sc in each corner, join with sl st in beg sc, turn.

Rnd 3: Ch 1, sc in first st, [sc in next st, ch 1] around with (sc, ch 1) twice in each center corner st, join with sl st in beg sc. Fasten off. ❏❏

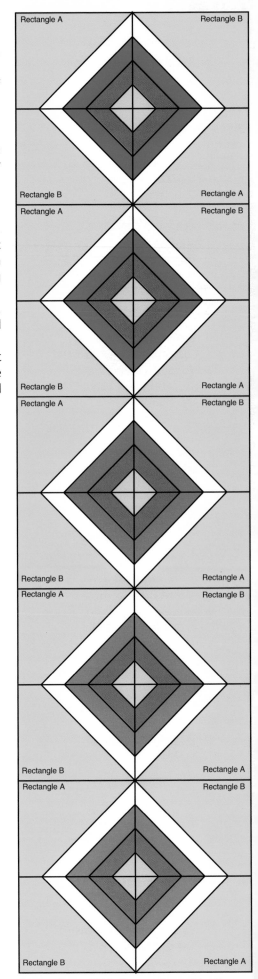

Sunny Shores Table Runner Assembly Diagram
Fig. 3

SKILL LEVEL

INTERMEDIATE

FINISHED SIZE

84 inches square

MATERIALS

❑ Red Heart Super Saver medium (worsted) weight yarn (7 oz/ 364 yds/198g per skein):

4 MEDIUM

7 skeins #528 medium purple

5 skeins #776 dark orchid

3 skeins each #312 black, #530 orchid and #579 pale plum

❑ Sizes G/6/4mm and H/8/5mm crochet hooks or size needed to obtain gauge

❑ Tapestry needle

GAUGE

Size H hook: Rows 1 & 2 = 1¾ inches

SPECIAL STITCHES

Beginning diagonal stitch (beg diagonal st): Ch 6, dc in 4th ch from hook *(first 3 chs count as first ch-3 sp)*, dc in each of last 2 chs *(see row 1 on Fig. 1)*.

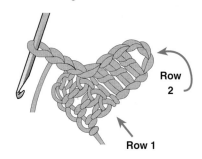

Diagonal Stitch
Fig. 1

Diagonal stitch (diagonal st): Sl st in next ch-3 sp *(see row 2 of Fig. 1)*, ch 3, 3 dc in same ch sp.

Beginning diagonal decrease (beg diagonal dec): Ch 3, 3 dc in same ch sp.

Invisible seam: Lay pieces to be joined edge to edge, with tapestry

needle, secure yarn at top of first piece *(see Fig. 2)*, [st in 2nd piece by going in and out of edge st, stitch in same way back in first piece] across. Secure end.

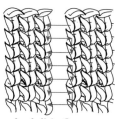

Invisible Seam
Fig. 2

INSTRUCTIONS

BEDSPREAD

SQUARE

Make 64.

Row 1: With size H hook and pale plum, **beg diagonal st** *(see Special Stitches)*, turn.

Row 2: Beg diagonal st, **diagonal st** *(see Special Stitches)*, turn. *(2 diagonal sts)*

Rows 3–6: Beg diagonal st, diagonal st in each diagonal st across, turn. At end of last row, fasten off. *(6 diagonal sts at end of last row)*

Row 7: Join medium purple with sl st in first st, beg diagonal st, diagonal st in each diagonal st across, turn. *(7 diagonal sts)*

Rows 8 & 9: Rep row 3. At end of last row, fasten off.

Row 10: With black, rep row 7. Fasten off. *(10 diagonal sts)*

Row 11: With dark orchid, rep row 7. *(11 diagonal sts)*

Row 12: Rep row 3. *(12 diagonal sts)*

Row 13: Sl st across to first ch sp, **beg diagonal dec** *(see Special Stitches)* in same ch sp, diagonal st in each diagonal st across, turn. Fasten off. *(11 diagonal sts)*

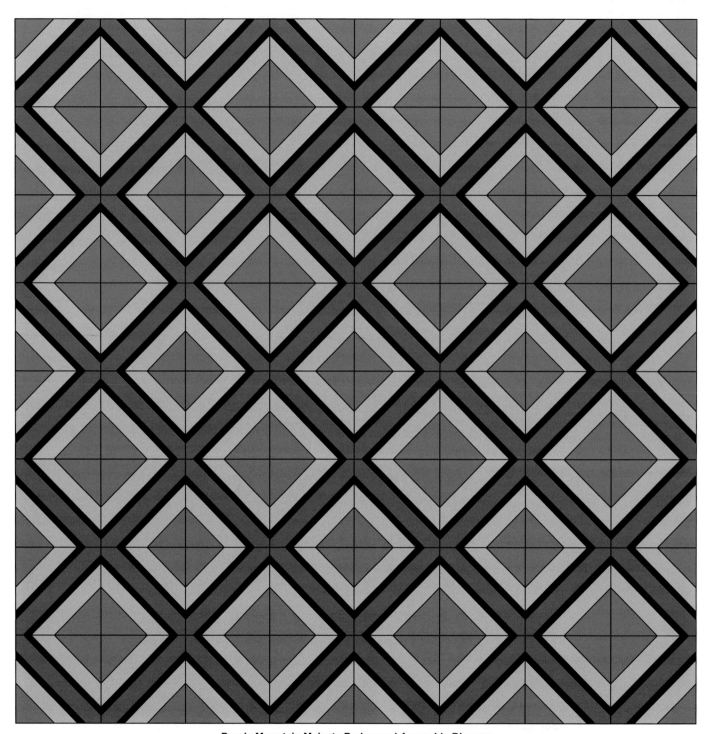

Purple Mountain Majesty Bedspread Assembly Diagram
Fig. 3

Row 14: Join black with sl st in ch sp of last diagonal st, beg diagonal dec in same ch sp, diagonal st in each diagonal st across, turn. Fasten off. *(10 diagonal sts)*

Row 15: With medium purple, rep row 14. *(9 diagonal sts)*

Rows 16 & 17: Sl st across to ch sp of last diagonal st, beg diagonal dec in same ch sp, diagonal st in each diagonal st across, turn. At end of last row, fasten off. *(7 diagonal sts at end of last row)*

Row 18: Join pale orchid with sl st in first ch sp, beg diagonal dec, diagonal st across to last diagonal st, sl st in ch sp of last diagonal st, turn. *(6 diagonal sts)*

Rows 19–22: Sl st in each of first 3 sts, diagonal st in each diagonal st across to last diagonal st, sl st in ch-3 sp of last diagonal st, turn. At end of last row, fasten off. *(2 diagonal sts at end of last row)*

Row 23: Sl st in each of first 3 sts, diagonal st in next diagonal st, sl st in ch-3 sp of last diagonal st. Fasten off.

ASSEMBLY

With matching color yarn using invisible seam *(see Special Stitches)*, sew tog according to Fig. 3.

EDGING

Rnd 1: With size H hook, join medium purple with sc in any corner st, 2 sc in same st, evenly sp sc around outer edge with 3 sc in each corner, join with sl st in beg sc, turn.

Rnd 2: Ch 1, sc in each st around, with 3 sc in each center corner st, join with sl st in beg sc, turn. Fasten off.

Rnd 3: Join dark orchid with sc in any center corner st, 2 sc in same st, sc in each st around, with 3 sc in each center corner st, join with sl st in beg sc, turn.

Rnd 4: Rep rnd 2.

Rnd 5: Join black with sc in any center corner st, 2 sc in same st, sc in each st around, with 3 sc in each center corner st, join with sl st in beg sc, **do not turn.**

Rnd 6: With size G hook, working from left to right, ch 1, **reverse sc** *(see Fig. 4)* in each st around, join with sl st in beg reverse sc. Fasten off. ❑❏

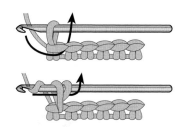

Reverse Single Crochet
Fig. 4

TOLL-FREE ORDER LINE or to request a free catalog (800) LV-ANNIE (800) 582-6643
Customer Service (800) AT-ANNIE (800) 282-6643, **Fax** (800) 882-6643
Visit anniesattic.com

We have made every effort to ensure the accuracy and completeness of these instructions.
We cannot, however, be responsible for human error, typographical mistakes or variations in individual work.

ISBN: 978-1-59635-180-6

Stitch Guide

ABBREVIATIONS

beg ....begin/beginning
bpdc ....back post double crochet
bpsc .... back post single crochet
bptr.............back post treble crochet
CC ....contrasting color
ch ....chain stitch
ch- ....refers to chain or space
   previously made (i.e., ch-1 space)
ch sp .... chain space
cl.. cluster
cm ....centimeter(s)
dc ....double crochet
dec..decrease/decreases/decreasing
dtr....................double treble crochet
fpdc ....front post double crochet
fpsc .... front post single crochet
fptr...............front post treble crochet
g .... gram(s)
hdc ....half double crochet
inc ......increase/increases/increasing
lp(s) ....loop(s)
MC ....main color
mm .... millimeter(s)
oz.....................................ounce(s)
pc .... popcorn
rem ....remain/remaining
rep .... repeat(s)
rnd(s) ....round(s)
RS...right side
sc................. single crochet
sk.................................skip(ped)
sl st ....slip stitch
sp(s)................................space(s)
st(s)..................................stitch(es)
tog ....together
tr.....................................treble crochet
trtr ....triple treble
WS................................. wrong side
yd(s).................................yard(s)
yo ....yarn over

Chain—ch: Yo, pull through lp on hook.

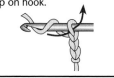

Slip stitch—sl st: Insert hook in st, yo, pull through both lps on hook.

Single crochet—sc: Insert hook in st, yo, pull through st, yo, pull through both lps on hook.

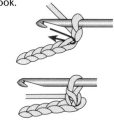

**Front loop—front lp
Back loop—back lp**

Front Loop   Back Loop

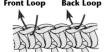

**Front post stitch—fp:
Back post stitch—bp:** When working post st, insert hook from right to left around post st on previous row.

Back   Front

Post of Stitch

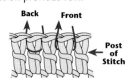

Half double crochet—hdc: Yo, insert hook in st, yo, pull through st, yo, pull through all 3 lps on hook.

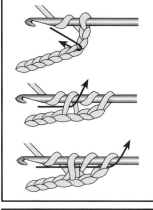

Double crochet—dc: Yo, insert hook in st, yo, pull through st, [yo, pull through 2 lps] twice.

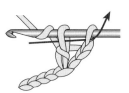

Change colors: Drop first color; with 2nd color, pull through last 2 lps of st.

Treble crochet—tr: Yo 2 times, insert hook in st, yo, pull through st, [yo, pull through 2 lps] 3 times.

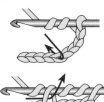

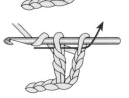

Double treble crochet—dtr: Yo 3 times, insert hook in st, yo, pull through st, [yo, pull through 2 lps] 4 times.

Single crochet decrease (sc dec): (Insert hook, yo, draw up a lp) in each of the sts indicated, yo, draw through all lps on hook.

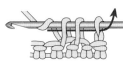

Example of 2-sc dec

Half double crochet decrease (hdc dec): (Yo, insert hook, yo, draw lp through) in each of the sts indicated, yo, draw through all lps on hook.

Example of 2-hdc dec

Double crochet decrease (dc dec): (Yo, insert hook, yo, draw lp through, yo, draw through 2 lps on hook) in each of the sts indicated, yo, draw through all lps on hook.

Example of 2-dc dec

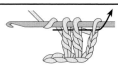

Example of 2-tr dec

Treble crochet decrease (tr dec): Holding back last lp of each st, tr in each of the sts indicated, yo, pull through all lps on hook.

US	UK
sl st (slip stitch)	= sc (single crochet)
sc (single crochet)	= dc (double crochet)
hdc (half double crochet)	= htr (half treble crochet)
dc (double crochet)	= tr (treble crochet)
tr (treble crochet)	= dtr (double treble crochet)
dtr (double treble crochet)	= ttr (triple treble crochet)
skip	= miss